The Monsters of Maumbury Rings

and
other poems for all ages

by John Barclay

with line drawings by Jim Housego

The Monsters of Maumbury Rings

Published by The Conrad Press in the United Kingdom 2023

Tel: +44(0)1227 472 874
www.theconradpress.com
info@theconradpress.com

ISBN 978-1-915494-38-2

Typesetting and Cover Design by: Charlotte Mouncey, www.bookstyle.co.uk
The Conrad Press logo was designed by Maria Priestley.

Printed and bound in Great Britain by Clays Ltd, Elcograf S.p.A.

INTRODUCTION

I am a performance poet; all my stuff is tried and tested. I wrote the poem *The Monsters of Maumbury Rings* to perform in the Dorchester Literary Festival in the grassy prehistoric henge known as Maumbury Rings. It went down well, despite a drum workshop starting up in the next tent. I was asked later to perform the poem at a sixtieth birthday party. One of the guests, a primary school teacher, asked me to write a poem about pirates*, the theme she'd chosen for her class of six-year-olds. This encouraged me to write further poems for children, but more and more I found that they were just as popular with adults. This gave me the idea of a book of poems for all ages.

I hope that, whatever your age, you'll enjoy them.

John Barclay - February 2023

---

*   'When the Pirates come'; see page 91.

Contents

The Monsters of Maumbury Rings

and
other poems for all ages

THE MONSTERS OF MAUMBURY RINGS

Elizabeth (staying in Penge* with her father)
said, 'What is the scariest thing you could meet?
Well, would it be ghosts, a fierce tiger or, rather,
a terrorist driving like mad down the street?'
Her dad said, 'The scariest creature that springs
to my mind's the Jeddle of Maumbury Rings.'

'The Jeddle, the Jeddle – but what do you mean?'
'A dangerous beast that has never been caught –
or photographed, Lizzie – although it's been seen,
but those who have done so were rendered distraught.
It's probably hearsay like so many things.
It's only been sighted at Maumbury Rings.

And just what it is, well, they haven't a clue.
It may not be real although rumours persist.
But no one has managed to get a clear view –
it only appears in the fog or the mist.'
'So when can we go to these mulberry things?'
'You're getting it wrong – they're called "Maumbury Rings".'

*   *in S E London*

'Well, Maumbury Rings – I don't know what they are.'
'A big oval bank that is known as a henge.'
'So when can we go to this henge – is it far?
Is there one in Bromley – or right here in Penge?'
'Oh, no, it's in Dorset. It's one of the things
I'd quite like to visit, the Maumbury Rings.'

'If you want to go, that makes two of us, Dad.
Let's go this weekend, while you've got me to stay.
We must take this chance – if we don't we'd be mad.'
'It's too far to go, Liz – I mean, for the day.
You'll just have to wait till I organise things
to go for a weekend to Maumbury Rings.'

'Elizabeth, darling, I've got some good news!'
her father announced over breakfast next day.
'I've talked to a friend of mine, Kevin King, whose
bungalow's empty. He says we can stay.
He's off with his rock group – plays keyboard and sings.
He lives only minutes from Maumbury Rings!'

'Oh, Daddy, that's wicked. I'll give you a medal!
Does that really mean that we're going today?
D'you think there's a chance we'll set eyes on the Jeddle?
I'm starting a project on it right away.
But first of all, Daddy, I'll get all my things.
We're off to the Jeddle of Maumbury Rings!'

The journey from Penge was a rather long haul
and nearing Bere Regis they ran into fog.
The traffic to Dorchester slowed to a crawl.
But throughout the journey the child was agog
with all the excitement that mystery brings –
and thoughts of the Jeddle of Maumbury Rings!

In darkening fog – and on foot in the end –
they managed to locate the rock singer's house.
'The Jeddle will find us!' Liz liked to pretend
and crept round the bungalow quiet as a mouse.
She found a guitar that had only five strings
and made up a song about Maumbury Rings.

'So when are we going?' she called to her dad.
He said, 'Well, my love, it's a hideous night . . . '
'Oh, no, Daddy, please – look, it isn't that bad.
In this fog we might just spot the Jeddle – we might!
And, Dad, have you seen how the fog sort of clings?
Just right for the Jeddle of Maumbury Rings!'

'Well, all right, Elizabeth, but understand –
on this sort of night you must do what I say,'
her father insisted. 'Hold onto my hand.
I'll give you the torch so we don't lose our way.'
'I think we're the bravest of soldiers – or kings!'
she squealed as they set off for Maumbury Rings.

They got there and climbed to the top of the bank.
They stood by a path that was slippery and steep,
and there in an atmosphere chilly and dank
the most they could see was the fog in a heap.
'I feel that we're flying without any wings!'
Elizabeth whispered on Maumbury Rings.

'Let's go down this footpath!' she suddenly cried,
and tugged on her father's hand, making him yell,
'Stop it, Elizabeth!' Starting to slide,
she let go his hand and the torch. Then she fell,
and, suffering the sort of abrasion that stings,
she shot to the bottom of Maumbury Rings.

She lay on the wet grass and started to cry.
Her tracksuit was drenched, she was cold and afraid.
She screamed for her daddy, and heard a reply.
It wasn't her father, but something that swayed
the way that the trunk of an elephant swings.
Yes, something was stirring in Maumbury Rings.

'I hope it's the Jeddle. I don't! Oh, I'm scared!'
she said to herself. Now aware of its size,
she managed to get to her feet and she stared,
but all she could see was the shape of its eyes,
and all she could hear was the animal's wings
collapsing and shaking in Maumbury Rings.

She felt its hot breath on the top of her head.
A stale sort of odour emerged from its snout.
She thought that in moments she'd find herself dead.
She opened her mouth but no sound would come out.
She noticed a pricking (like jellyfish stings)
in both of her eyes there on Maumbury Rings.

The monster bent down and announced in her ear,
'If you were a grown-up, I'd teach you to meddle,
but as you're a child, you 'ave nothing to fear,
I'm lifting you up for a ride,' said the Jeddle.
''twill feel like a tractor without any springs.
We'll do a whole circuit of Maumbury Rings.'

It opened its jaws and took hold of her waist.
Elizabeth just didn't know what to do.
Then, lifting her high, the animal placed
her onto its back, like a ride in the zoo.
'Cling tight to my fur and don't tug on my wings!'
it cried as they bumped over Maumbury Rings.

'And now do you think I am scary – or what?'
it asked her. She said, 'I'm afraid I don't know
just yet, Mr Jed, if you're scary or not . . . '
'I'm scary all right, although not like the Vho.
The Vho is the worst of the scarier things,'
admitted the Jeddle of Maumbury Rings.

And . . . that's all we've time for. I'm putting you down,'
the Jeddle explained, 'because now I must go.
I've very few seconds to get out of town.
I sense the arrival, my dear, of the Vho!'
And this was the scariest of all the things
Elizabeth learnt – there on Maumbury Rings.

Then, trying to hide herself under the fog,
her quivering face she pressed into the grass.
She shuddered and whimpered – or yelped liked a dog –
and prayed that each nightmarish second would pass;
but time beat as slow as a pendulum swings.
She thought she would die there on Maumbury Rings.

And that's where he found her – her father, I mean –
still breathing, of course, but she felt a year older.
'Elizabeth, darling, oh where have you been?'
her father implored. 'I was desperate,' he told her.
'Oh, Daddy! Dear Daddy! Such terrible things
have left me so frightened on Maumbury Rings!'

He gave her a mug of her favourite soup
when back at the bungalow. Tucked up in bed,
she played a CD made by Kevin King's group.
Though raucous and strident, Elizabeth said,
'It will help me to settle. And if Mummy rings
please try not to tell about Maumbury Rings.

She'll just have to wait till I get back to Penge
and finish these projects I've got on the go.
The first is 'The Jeddle that Lives in the Henge'.
The second one's called 'The Return of the Vho',
a hideous monster that frightens <u>all things</u>
and scares off the Jeddle of Maumbury Rings.'

Elizabeth went with her father next day
to look for the torch and examine the Henge.
There wasn't a sign of the monsters' foray.
But Kevin King helped Liz to get her revenge
by writing a song for her that she still sings,
'The Menacing Monsters of Maumbury Rings' –
. . . The Monsters of Maumbury
Rings!

ADULTS

Adults are clever and know lots of stuff;
and if they're not sure, well, they know how to bluff.
They talk about everything under the sun,
but, unlike us children, they never have fun.

They talk about things in a showing-off way,
say, 'That's all it takes at the end of the day'.
They go on for centuries once they've begun,
but, unlike us children, they never have fun.

They know the expression for this and for that,
say, 'Feline's the word you should use for a cat'
and 'Fabric is woven while fibres are spun,'
but, unlike us children, they never have fun.

They go out to meetings, ask questions, discuss.
They fret or complain and create a big fuss.
They know more or less how the Country is run,
but, unlike us children, they never have fun.

They work to earn money and buy the big things;
they like the importance that owning them brings.
They know the best method to get something done,
but, unlike us children, they never have fun.

They fly to strange places, some far, far away –
across the Atlantic in less than a day.
They know how to bake a cinnamon bun,
but, unlike us children, they never have fun.

They like to play games, they jog, they 'work out'.
They 'go to the football', they drink and they shout.
They cannot be happy unless their team's won
and, unlike us children, they never have fun.

They talk of the weather we're having that day.
They say, 'Take a mac,' when the sky's looking grey.
They laugh and they joke – they enjoy a good pun,
but they never go in for what we would call fun.

ALBATROSS

tireless albatross
air-dancing across the wake
lets the ship go first

BLINDINGLY OBVIOUS

I've had it up to here with Christmas lights!
Don't get me wrong – I like those in the town.
They cheer us up on dreary winter nights,
gracing the streets as jewels grace a crown.

It's not communal efforts that I curse,
but unchecked individual enterprise –
the clown who swathes his house in lights. What's worse,
he leaves them on all night to plague our eyes.

I live in Cranborne Crescent – number two,
and opposite my house, at number one,
the Hunter-Dobsons lurk, a desperate crew
hell-bent, it seems, on rivalling the sun.

They've decked their bungalow with flashing lights,
including carport, garden shed and hedge,
while high above these down-to-earth delights
eight flying reindeer draw a giant sledge.

It's driven by a mighty Santa Claus,
who waves at me ten thousand times a night.
His bulging sack of toys, without a pause,
glows white, blue, green, then back again to white.

As if that weren't enough, at number three
the 'pious' Jacksons – not to be outdone –
have mounted an entire Nativity
to trump the Hunter-Ds at number one.

In line with this ambitious stratagem,
they've flashing shepherds tending flashing sheep,
a flashing stable, big as Bethlehem.
The Infant doesn't flash – that would look cheap!

And while my wanton neighbours warm the sky,
consuming four months' fuel in a night,
I draw my flimsy curtains with a sigh
and turn to face the wall to save my sight.

I'd like to call at numbers three and one.
'I've come to read the meter,' I'd explain,
and while their backs were turned I'd think it fun
to disconnect these blighters at the main.

But, as it is the season of goodwill,
I won't do anything that might cause fights,
though, while I do not wish these dear folk ill,
I've had it up to here with Christmas lights!

———

EVERYONE'S AN ODDITY

Everyone's peculiar, even little Julia,
coz I heard that Julia was born at sea.
Everyone's extraordinary; none of 'em is ordinary.
Everyone's an oddity – apart from me!

Some do funny things because of their religion.
Ethan sent a message by a homing pigeon.
Maria Alvarado comes from Guatemala.
Natasha Wilson's mother runs a beauty parlour.
Darren Fletcher's home is now a caravan.
Melanie Jerome is living with her nan.
All of them extraordinary; none of 'em is ordinary.
Everyone's an oddity – apart from me!

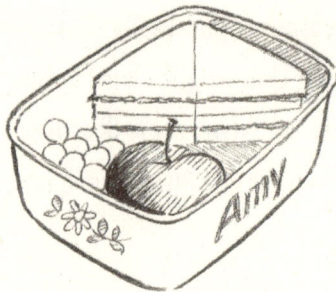

Jamil has an artificial eye.

Hannah's father used to be a spy.

Ellie has a birthmark on her face.

Etinosa wears a dental brace.

Gail can play the cello and the harp.

Gowon has a knife that's very sharp.

All of them extraordinary; none of 'em is ordinary.

Everyone's an oddity – apart from me!

Callum Clark is a hefty bruiser.

Megan Jones is a wheelchair user.

Kati is Hungarian,

Roger's vegetarian.

Amy brings in sandwiches.

Luke can speak four languages.

All of them extraordinary; none of 'em is ordinary.

Everyone's an oddity – apart from me!

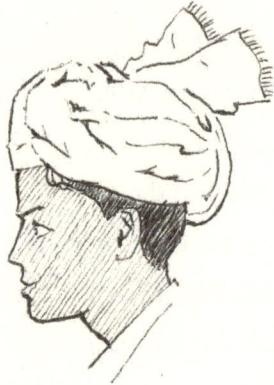

Gugu comes from Durban.

Mahesh wears a turban.

Joy gets coughing fits.

Neil can do the splits.

Yamu's from Nepal, and

Yubi's very small.

All of them extraordinary; none of 'em is ordinary.

Everyone's an oddity – apart from me!

Ohhhhh – I'm feeling out of it;
I think I'm going to shout a bit –
Everyone's an oddity – apart from me –
the only one who's ordinary!
Isn't that extraordinary?
Everyone an oddity apart from me!

That makes me extraordinary – so, I'm far from ordinary!
Everyone's an oddity – including me! . . . Ugh!
Now I'm feeling rotten, coz I'd quite forgotten –
I'm not a human child at all – I'm a chimpanzee!

ele

HOMO NOT SO SAPIENS

What an animal is man –
does so much because he can,
makes his habitat fantastic,
full of concrete, glass and plastic,
poison, noise 'n' rising seas,
melts the ice caps, fells the trees,
carves the land up into pieces,
wipes out species after species,
knows the planet's fragile state –
does too little far too late.

HOW THE TURKEY COOKED MY GOOSE

Adapted from an anonymous poem found on the Internet

The turkey shot out of the oven
and rocketed into the air.
It smashed a glass jug on the table
and nearly demolished a chair.

Like dynamite blasting a quarry,
it burst with a deafening boom,
then spattered all over the kitchen,
transforming the look of the room.

It ruined my favourite cookbook.
It fouled the whipped cream in the bowl.
There wasn't a way I could stop it –
that turkey was out of control!

It coated the walls and the windows.
It spread out all over the floor.
There were pieces of flesh on the ceiling,
recalling the horrors of war.

We made do with boiled eggs, cold herrings,
the sprouts, some defrosted white bread
and, with burgundy no longer fitting,
the stock from the giblets instead.

Reclaiming the kitchen took ages.
I said to myself as I mopped,
'I'll never again stuff a turkey
with popcorn that hasn't been popped!'

POOLE AND HER LIGHTHOUSE

Here in Poole, this ancient port,
long a holiday resort,
shoppers swarm the level crossing,
sailboats in the Harbour tossing,
water sports to watch or try,
as back and forth the ferries ply.
Visitors explore the Quay,
view the famous pottery.

Poole is Bournemouth's older sister,
just as bright without the glister –
with her gleaming, on-shore Lighthouse,
cultural beacon, quite the right house
for the BSO and all the arts –
coachloads come from many parts.
See the building, oh so cool,
when at dusk it lights up Poole.

RECYCLING THE CYCLE OF SPIKY MIKE SYKES

I'm cycling off to recycle this cycle.
I'm doing it solely since my buddy Michael
entrusted me with the care of his bike,
once ridden with joy by my spiky friend Mike.

We all called him 'Spiky' and said, 'crikey, Mikey!'
My spiky friend Mikey replied, 'Don't say, 'crikey!'
I've lacquered my hair to stick up in a spike!
It's my head of hair – I can do what I like,

and I cling to cycling like shorts to the thigh cling.
My eye-catching spike is a badge of my cycling.'
When wet, the spike glistened like scales on a pike
and stood so erect it was rhino-horn-like.

He looked like a Viking – the likeness was striking.
The bike and the spike were so much to Mike's liking,
he showed off his spike every time he went biking
and sharpened the spike for some bold balloon spiking.

Then Mike sped as fast as a fork-lightning strike,
but kingfisher-like he dived into a dyke.
The cycle survived this and so did poor Mike,
although he was caught by a tyke* in the dyke.

Mike's spike and the rest of his head hair alike,
sheered off from his scalp and was lost in the dyke.
Now, I ride his bike; even push it, for Mikey,
who's no longer known by his old nickname 'Spiky'?

I'm off to recycle, for Michael, his bike.
I'm taking a new route avoiding the dyke.
I can't cycle back coz I won't have the bike –
the journey on foot is one helluva hike.

* 'Tyke' is an old word for a dog. 'Ike' was the nickname of
Dwight Eisenhower, who, before becoming the 34th President of
the United States of America, played an important role for the
Allies in the Second World War.

But, hang on a minute, would one of you like
to save me the job of recycling this bike?
Will somebody buy it, an historic cycle,
which used to belong to my spiky friend Michael?

The money I get in the bargain we strike
will let me buy something essential for Mike,
a wig for his baldness. I'm sure he would like
no longer to look like President Ike.

SILLY SOPPY SAUSAGES

zip-a-dee zip-a-dee zoo
bongo b'tongo boo and
silly soppy sausages too

zip-a-dee zip-a-dee zoo
bongo b'tongo boo
clacker man packer man
long lost lacquer man
silly soppy sausages too

zip-a-dee zip-a-dee zoo
bongo b'tongo boo
clacker man packer man
long lost lacquer man
bodger boy wonder boy
dodger boy thunder boy
silly soppy sausages too

zip-a-dee zip-a-dee zoo
bongo b'tongo boo
clacker man packer man
long lost lacquer man
bodger boy wonder boy
dodger boy thunder boy
jolly Molly bossable
potty Polly possible
silly soppy sausages too

zip-a-dee zip-a-dee zoo
bongo b'tongo boo
clacker man packer man
long lost lacquer man
bodger boy wonder boy
dodger boy thunder boy
jolly Molly bossable
potty Polly possible
physical phenomenon
Philippa went on and on
silly soppy sausages too
silly soppy sausages – pow!

———

THE CAFÉ OLÉ

At the Café Olé, you can get crème brulée
with a crust so robust you could skate on it.
Their seafood ragôut they serve red, white and blue,
with a Prince-of-Wales biscuit to grate on it.
They've mustard & cress, but their custard's a mess;
you would think it was made by a horse.
But the dish I like most is their 'jelly on toast',
which they swamp with a yummy rum sauce.

At the Café Olé, you can order today
your cauliflower soup for next year,
But sadly somehow if you want the stuff now
you can just go and whistle, I fear.
The management hope that the tables all slope
so the food will end up on the floor,
when a Labrador pup comes and gobbles it up,
then performs a quick dance to get more.

At the Café Olé, though you don't have to pay,
you do have to smile – they insist!
If you're sullen or pout, they will bundle you out,
then they enter your name on a list.
And if you go back they will chide you and smack
you with rhubarb or celery stalks.
And, whether you mind or not, you will find
yourself taking the puppy for walks.

At the Café Olé, I am sorry to say
that, whenever his 'Roux' isn't thickening,
the chef has recourse (when he's making a sauce)
to practices you would find sickening.
The waitresses may sometimes carry a tray
but you'll find that more often they're dropping 'em.
They like to have fun throwing fruit or a bun –
once they start this there's no hope of stopping 'em.

At the Café Olé, they go out of their way
to <u>prevent</u> people feeling at ease.
While you sit there for hours admiring the flowers,
the staff come and go as they please.
The sight of some bloke (with a globe artichoke
impaled in his throat) turning blue –
they will greet with a shout, handing camcorders out,
and tip <u>more</u> artichokes in the stew!

At the Café Olé, they do things their own way –
such behaviour's unheard of in France.
The chef cannot cook but you still have to book –
oh – at <u>least</u> seven months in advance.
It's their dandelion juice and the tireless abuse
that have made it the top spot in town.
So hurry along before something goes wrong
and you find that they've closed the place down!

ℓ

THE EARWIG IN MY PENCIL CASE

The earwig in my pencil case
enjoys its smell of wood.
I'll take my little friend to school –
he's promised to be good.

The gecko on my bedroom wall,
her bulging eye on me,
waits till I've gone to sleep and then
her friends come round for tea.

The jackdaw is my latest pet.
I'm teaching him to talk.
I'm going to make a lead for him
and take him for a walk.

My badger's started burrowing,
a hole beneath my bed.
One day, at breakfast we'll look up
and see her stripy head.

The leopard in my dressing gown
(he wears it when he stays)
flies in from far Namibia.
He's often here for days.

The warthog in our garden pond
came in to have a drink.
We had to shut the windows coz
he gave out such a stink.

An elephant's too big for here.
I keep mine in the park.
She's done a lot of damage there
and scares folk when it's dark.

I wish that I lived near the sea,
so I could learn to sail.
I'd offer lifts to seals I met
and get to know a whale.

THE IRON BALL

An iron ball
stood on a wall
at Hartstop Hall
and persons all
both short and tall
came to the wall
to see the ball,
which through it all
o'ertopped the wall
and did not fall.

A lad named Saul
from Hartstop Hall
(a fathom tall
as I recall),
who had the gall
to scale the wall,
did heave and haul
upon the ball,
which, 'spite of all,
clave to the wall,
a stubborn ball
that would not fall.

So with a call
he summoned Paul
from out the Hall
(a child so small
he could but crawl)
and headstrong Saul
transported Paul,
wrapped in a shawl,
and did install
him on the wall,
whereat young Paul
began to crawl
along the wall
towards the ball.

Just then a squall
disturbed poor Paul.
(This will appal
you one and all.)
He chanced to fall
from off the wall.
I saw him sprawl
in death's cold thrall,
and haughty Saul
began to bawl.
He wrapped the small
corpse in the shawl
and carried Paul
to Hartstop Hall,
leaving the ball
upon the wall.

When darkness fell,
a maid called Nell
began to yell
and ring a bell.
The ball, it fell
and rolled pell-mell
towards a well,
wherein it fell.
There still it lies,
a worthless prize.
And that is all
about the ball.

THEIR VERY OWN ISLAND

Gregory Whiteside
looked on the bright side,
whatever befell him in life.
Becoming redundant
he saw as abundant
good fortune for him and his wife.

He said to his wife,
'Now, Lily, my life,
we don't have to hang around here.
We could go on a cruise –
whatever we choose.
Well, what would you like, Lily dear?'

She fondled his leg
and said, 'Dearest Greg,
I've harboured a dream for a while.
I thought it was mad
till I spotted this ad.
I'll show you – get ready to smile.

There's an island for sale
off Cornwall, near Hayle –
for seventy-five thousand pounds –
that's ever so cheap –
with forty-one sheep
and a cottage within its own grounds.

Now that would be grand.
We'd live off the land,
and you could catch fish in the sea.
I'd do the cooking.
There's no harm in looking.'
and Gregory said, 'I agree.

We could sell all we've got
and put it with what
I'm getting as severance pay.
Our very own island! –
We wanted to buy land.
Let's ring up the agent today.'

To avoid disappointment,
they made an appointment
to view it together next day.
They flew in a chopper.
The bill was a whopper,
but Lily was happy to pay.

Her heart gave a leap
on seeing the sheep
running away from the 'copter.
They started to bleat.
'Ah, don't they look sweet?'
said Lily, and nobody stopped her.

Greg liked the jetty.
The cottage was pretty
and Lil' loved the four-poster bed.
'The contract's prepared,'
the agent declared.
'You just have to sign here,' he said.

The move was a doddle.
'I'm sure something odd'll
occur very soon,' muttered Lil.
But once they'd unpacked
they began to react
to the atmosphere, dreamy and still.

After eight days
of euphoric haze,
the pair, as they stood at the door,
were startled to see
a boat on the quay
and a man in a suit step ashore.

'My name is John Peck.
I've come for your cheque.
I'm afraid it's that time of the year –
terribly boring,
the annual mooring
fee – four thousand pound odd, I fear.'

'Oh, heavens! Oh, heck!'
said Whiteside to Peck,
'We haven't a penny to spare.
I ask you to note
we don't have a boat.
It doesn't seem terribly fair.'

'Look, Mr Whiteside,
I'd stay on the right side
of the law – they can always enforce it.
I think you've ignored,
this island is moored –
towed here in April from Dorset.'

Then Lily burst out,
'I don't mean to shout,
but this is too much to endure.
Look, please, Mr Peck,
just hold on a sec',
for we own the freehold, I'm sure.'

'You own the top bit,
the bought-in-a-shop bit,
the pontoon-like polythene tray;
but four metres down
it belongs to the Crown.
To moor here, you have, ma'am, to pay.'

Lil' saw then what he meant,
'We signed an agreement –
there's nothing in there about this!'
'Just take a squint, ma'am,
at all the small print, ma'am.
There's no need to take it amiss.'

Then Greg said: 'I mean
we haven't a bean –
unless we can pay you in sheep.
Look, cast us adrift.
we'll just have to shift
for ourselves as we can on the deep.'

'If you don't pay, sir,
we'll tow you away, sir.
There's others who're waiting to moor.
The Norwegian Sea –
you can moor there for free.
They call it 'the Sea of the Poor'.

Then, giving a shrug,
he added, 'the tug
will work out at eight pound a mile.
It's cheaper to stay.
You've one month to pay.'
He left with a sickening smile.

Well, Lily was tearful,
but Greg remained cheerful.
'Never forget, I'm a Whiteside.
Whatever the weather
we'll still be together.
We've just got to look on the bright side.

I'll slaughter a ewe –
would be nice in a stew,
or if you prefer you can roast it.
It's all for the best –
our venture's progressed,
I'll open a bottle to toast it.'

'Oh don't kill a sheep –
I've still got a heap
of tins I can use in the hall.'
'Soon we'll be free, love,'
said Greg, 'Wait and see, love -
we'll have that world cruise after all.

I fancy the notion
of wand'rin' the ocean.
I'm sick of the peace and the quiet.
And luckily I've
always wanted to dive –
I'll go under the isle and untie it.'

He went underneath,
the hose in his teeth,
the better to breathe under water.
He managed to tackle
a very large shackle,
one taking more strain than it oughta.

His wrist getting sore,
he unscrewed some more,
until he had freed the last chain.
He carelessly chose
by means of the hose
to pull himself back up again.

The hose came adrift.
Decidedly miffed,
Greg swam to the surface to find
that, rushing headlong
in tidal flow strong,
the island had left him behind.

Meanwhile at the sink,
the lights on the blink,
the crockery put on a show.
A grapefruit went bowling.
The tins started rolling.
'I hope Greg's okay down below!'

Then Lily rushed out
and started to shout,
'Gregory, are you all right?'
The sheep acted silly,
and so did poor Lily.
Her husband was nowhere in sight.

But Greg, like a Whiteside,
still looked on the bright side,
thought, 'Water's quite warm for a dip!'
The light slowly dimming,
the brave Greg kept swimming,
while scanning the waves for a ship.

At quarter to one
as if it were fun
he finally struggled to land.
He crawled up the beach
too knackered for speech
and collapsed in a heap on the sand.

While most of the night,
as seabirds took fright,
the island continued to hurtle.
A cross-current fluky
then washed it to Newquay.
It floated ashore like a turtle.

Now Gregory, dazed
and cold – but not fazed –
sought help at a caravan site.
A couple called Smee
gave him clothes, cups of tea
and offered a bed for the night.

But Greg couldn't wait
to discover the fate
of the island abducting his Lily.
And thanks to the Smees
he reached the Police
at Redruth and drove them all silly.

His wife in a daze
had managed to raise
the coastguard, who mounted a search.
The sheep swam ashore,
began to explore,
and eight ended up in the church.

The police at Redruth
tried to get at the truth,
believing poor Whiteside deranged.
But somebody called
in, sounding appalled,
to say that the coastline had 'changed'.

In consequence, then
a car full of men
with Gregory drove to the coast.
On the four-poster bed
lay Lil', looking dead,
when Greg wandered in like a ghost.

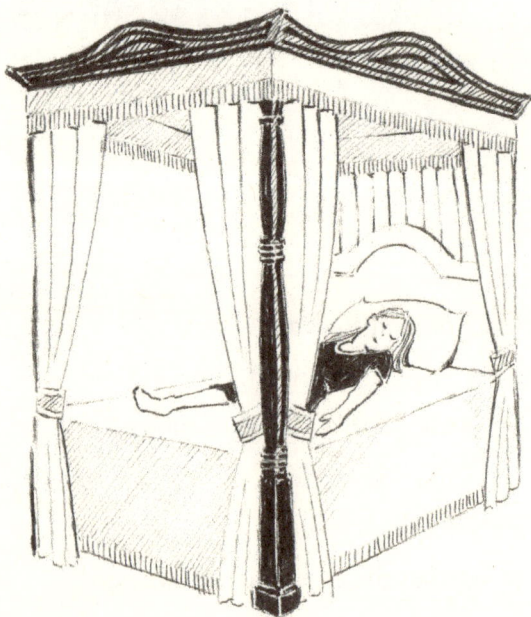

The Sunday Express
paid out in excess
of four thousand pounds for the venture.
The island was bought
by a dodgy consort-
-ium running a tax-haven venture.

The Whitesides remained
naïve, and retained
an outlook both trusting and plucky.
They ventured to rent
an igloo in Kent.
They're happy – well, happy-go-lucky.

It's not in my mind
a lesson to find,
but quoting brave Gregory Whiteside,
'This tale has a moral –
be loving, don't quarrel,
and steadfastly look on the bright side.'

THE POETRY COMPETITION

Ten little entrants trying hard to shine –
one didn't read the rules and then there were nine.
Nine little entrants working very late –
one suffered eye strain and then there were eight.
Eight little entrants one of them called Evan –
he penned his stuff in Welsh and then there were seven.
Seven little entrants living in the Styx –
one became a hermit and then there were six.
Six little entrants eager to survive –
one plagiarized the judge and then there were five.
Five little entrants mad on metaphor –
one overused the figure and then there were four.
Four little entrants daring as could be –
one wrote a screenplay and then there were three.
Three little entrants aiming at haiku –
one used twenty syllables and then there were two.
Two little entrants believing that they'd won –
one forgot the entrance fee and then there was one.
One little entrant had a lot of fun
knocking up <u>this</u> poem, then found that they'd <u>won!</u>

THE SCHOOL OUTING

We went on a special school outing
packed into an old orange bus.
Once it started, we all began shouting.
Miss Sharma said, 'Don't make a fuss!'

The vehicle shook us like punch bags.
The back of my neck became sore.
The Scott twins were sick in their lunch bags;
Rihanna was sick on the floor.

One of the windows kept rattling
and Rosalie hated the din.
To silence the noise she kept battling,
until a bold pigeon flew in.

Two of the girls started shrieking.
Tim gave it biscuits to munch,
then yelled out, 'This grape juice is leaking.
It's sloshing all over my lunch!'

The lions around Nelson's Column
made one of the boys give a cheer.
Miss Potcher stood up looking solemn
and said they were 'nothing to fear'.

The British Museum's enormous –
not hard for the driver to find.
Poor Ben was asleep like a dormouse.
I thought we would leave him behind.

The stuff in glass cases was boring.
The best were the Sphinx, the dead mummies –
and daddies, of course – not ignoring
the Buddhas with spherical tummies.

When Ben, the young dormouse, went missing
they locked us all up in a room.
'He's silly!' Miss Potcher kept hissing,
'expect he's asleep on a tomb!'

Going home, the bus stopped completely.
We'd to wait to be saved in the dark.
Miss Sharma began singing sweetly.
We sang the wrong tune for a lark.

The substitute bus was much smaller.
I sat on Miss Brassington's lap.
I asked, 'Is your name really Paula?'
She said, 'I can't give you a slap.'

My father who'd come to collect me
complained that he'd not had his tea.
'I hope it was worth it!' he muttered,
'Oh yes, Dad, the best it could be!'

THE STUDENT VOLUNTEER

The village was the home of almost
every sort of folk –
the studious, the curious,
the apathetic bloke,

the show-off and the wise guy,
the ever-busy bod,
the helpful ones, the stay-at-homes,
the sloth, the lazy clod,

the boozers and the gossips,
the hermit and the sick,
the critics and the nit-pickers,
the drummer with his stick,

the elders and the 'loud one',
the creeps, the hangers-on,
reporters from the local press,
and several men called 'John'.

The village hall had been blown down,
inviting ridicule.
The village elders called a meeting
in the village school.

They fixed a notice on a tree.
The drummer beat his drum.
The gossips spread the urgent news
that everyone should come.

The day arrived. The folk did too,
except those sick in bed,
the hermit and the 'stay-at-homes',
who stayed at home instead.

The apathetic stayed away,
the boozers sought a bar.
The sloth was loath to stir his stumps.
The show-off cleaned his car.

The curious were there in force,
the creeps and hangers-on,
reporters from the local press
and all the men called 'John'.

The oldest elder made a speech.
'The time has come,' he stressed,
'for everyone to play their part
and give their very best.

Now, as you know, our village hall
is lying on its side.
We've got to get it up again
to save our village pride.'

'I'll run the show,' the loud one said,
'if others do the work.'
The wise guy made some snide remarks,
and some began to smirk.

The critics all were critical,
and said, 'It can't be done.'
The nit-pickers picked lots of holes.
Support? They offered none.

'I'd <u>like</u> to help,' the busy bod
announced, 'but just now I'm
afraid I'm fully occupied
and haven't got the time.'

'I did so much last year,' said one,
'it's someone else's turn.'
'Don't look at me,' another cried,
'I've got a crust to earn.'

'Hold on!' the oldest elder cried,
'no one else should speak
unless they're going to help – or else,
it's going to take all week!'

The crowd fell silent. One or two
folk bowed their heads in shame.
Just then a student at the back
stood up and said her name.

'I'm not sure if I've got the skills,
I'm rather young, I fear,
but no one seems to want the job,
so I will volunteer.'

'We'll help you,' cried the helpful ones,
'it's much too much for you,
especially as there will be jobs
you won't know how to do.'

The oldest elder thanked them all
and said, 'It now appears
we can restore the village hall –
we have some volunteers.'

The student and her little band
began without delay
to list what needed to be done,
which filled them with dismay.

She called upon the sea cadets
to right the toppled hall
and then she planned the other jobs,
the big stuff and the small.

The busybody lent some tools,
the wise guy gave advice.
The loud one said, 'Just use my name.'
The creeps said, 'Ooh, that's nice!'

The curious turned up to watch,
the hangers-on to cheer.
The little band toiled bravely on
the best part of a year.

At last they cleaned the windows,
stuck posters on the wall.
The oldest elder said, 'We'll throw
a party in the hall.'

The usual fellers stayed away.
The usual suspects came.
'The village has regained her pride,'
the loud one could declaim.

The drummer once more banged the drum.
The sloth fell out of bed.
'What's all the stupid fuss about?'
the apathetic said.

Reporters took some photographs.
The boozers ran a bar.
The wise guy said 'I knew we could –
it looks quite good so far.'

'They had to bring the navy in!'
one critic then complained.
A nit-picker declared the floor
was only partly stained.

The lazy clod then ambled in.
'You know I sprained my toe –
well, it's much better now,' he said,
'I could have helped, you know.'

The creeps said, 'We've been right behind
the project all the year.'
The elders said, 'We thought it best
if we don't interfere.'

'It proves,' the oldest elder claimed,
'that when we're in a spot,
if the village works as one,
we can achieve a lot.'

'My team were great,' the student cried.
'You others have a nerve!
We bust ourselves to save your hall.
It's more than you deserve.

We volunteers did, oh, so much;
what you guys did was puny!'
I've learned a lot,' she said, 'and now
I'm going off to uni'.'

And then I'll help Ukrainians
who've suffered war and pillage.
Such folk are glad of any help –
unlike those in this village!'

'Hold on,' the oldest elder cried,
'I'm sorry you feel slighted.
We value what you've done for us –
no need to get excited.

And now I call on everyone
to give three hearty cheers
for you, who led the project, and
your team of volunteers!

And, when we've paid off all the bills,
our duty we won't shirk,
for we will start a special fund
to help finance your work.'

THE UNWANTED VISITOR

If I'd known you were coming I'd have baked a cake
of duckweed and garbage out of the lake.
You say that you came here by mistake,
so why'd you wriggle in like a sneaky snake?

If I'd known you were coming I'd have locked the door
and hid in the shed or at number four,
coz I can't forget, when you came before,
you bore the very hallmark of a crushing bore.

If I'd known you were coming I'd have said, 'You can't!
I've got to purchase a potted plant
and post it off to a poorly aunt.'
If you think that I'll forgive you, too bad – I shan't.

But, now you're here and there is no cake,
go on, sit down for goodness sake.
I'll do my best to stay awake,
while you tell me one … more … time … that you can't eat steak.

———

TO A NEW GRANDMOTHER

No one can order a grandchild.
Once you had borne children,
for years all you could do
was patiently wait, nursing
a secret hope. So, now that
the wondrous, wished-for parcel
has safely arrived, you will
count it as a boon.

You and your daughter are equal,
both of you mothers now,
the two of you more in tune.
You know what it means to your child
to cuddle a child of her own.
You know too the joys,
the broken nights, the worries,
the dramas that lie ahead.

But you are the luckier mother
for you have the better deal.
Yours is a part-time role –
just helping out. Yet you
and the child will share a hotline,
by-passing family tensions.
You'll watch her flourish and grow –
somebody new in your life.

—❧—

Young and old members of the community of the town of Wareham (in Dorset) came together to make a tree out of clay, each leaf celebrating the life of the person who fashioned it. I wrote the following poem to mark the completion of the tree and its 'planting' in the library garden.

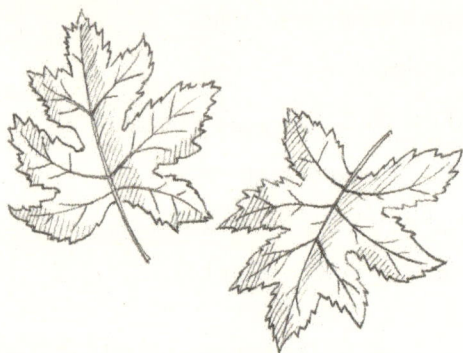

TREES

Gentle, long-living giants,
purifying our air,
sheltering birds and beetles,
bearing fruit, giving shade,
soft carpets of leaves,
places to hide, climb and play.
Seedlings, saplings and sturdy trunks,
young and old can grow together.

We have made a tree
of clay – bark and leaves
shaped and decorated
by children and seniors
working side by side,
so that here in this garden,
book-lovers and visitors,
young and old, will smile together.

We want our tree to flourish,
branch out, bear fruit –
not apples or chestnuts,
but new ideas that are fun
for both generations
to try – so that,
sharing these things,
young and old may bloom together.

WHAT ARE TUMMY BUTTONS FOR?

I know what ears and legs are for,
and hearts and elbows too.
But why do we have tummy buttons?
'can't think what <u>they</u> do.

Well, are they like the buttons on
the cuffs of Daddy's suit?
Coz they're just decoration,
to make the suit look cute.

Perhaps they're like the button in
the middle of a cushion,
holding in the cover for
the stuffing stuff to push on.

Lizzie says that babies have them
in the mummy's tummy,
so the child can feed on blood
it takes in from its mummy.

But babies aren't mosquitoes;
and milk's what babies like.
You might as well say Santa Claus
gets here by motorbike.

Daddy said that Liz was right
and then we went online,
to try and find a diagram
that would 'explain it fine'.

But, though we found the diagram,
I'm still a bit confused.
It hasn't solved the problem –
but it kept us all amused.

—

WHEN ARE YOU GOING TO DIE, GREAT-GRANNY?

When are you going to die, Great-granny?
When are you going to die?
Look, I may not get over this silly disease,
but I'm jolly well going to try.

But when are you going to die, Great-granny?
When are you going to die?
Well, it won't be this afternoon, my sweet –
I'm making a gooseberry pie.

When are you going to die, Great-granny -
when you've stopped having fun?
I think you're forgetting my age, little angel -
I'm only just ninety-one.

When you finally die, Great-granny,
will you be buried – or burnt?
I really don't care – I'll be past it by then.
That's one of the things that I've learnt.

When you're no longer with us, Great-granny,
what are we going to do?
You're all going to manage things perfectly well.
Now, which of the twenty are you?

I'm Lennie from Lulworth, remember, Great-granny?
So, when is it going to be?
I was thinking of Saturday week, little poppet –
if everyone's going to be free.

WHEN THE PIRATES COME

Yo, ho, ho and a bottle of rum!
Let's all hide when the pirates come.
From our tree house roof, I hope,
we'll see them through our telescope.
If we're quiet they won't hear us,
even if they come quite near us.

Yo, ho, ho and a bottle of rum!
We can watch the pirates come.
The captain's name, I think, is Jack.
His hair is long; his beard is black.
He wears a patch across his eye.
His blue tattoo says, 'Do or Die!'

Yo, ho, ho and a bottle of rum!
No one move as the pirates come!
That one's nose looks like a carrot.
On his shoulder there's a parrot.
Do you think the bird can talk?
Or does it only squeak and squawk?

Yo, ho, ho and a bottle of rum!
Not a sound now! Here they come.
One of them has got a scar
across his face, shaped like a car.
His left arm's horrid – oh, don't look.
He's got no hand – there's just a hook!

Yo, ho, ho and a bottle of rum!
We all saw the pirates come.
Soon we'll watch these eight fierce men
row back to their ship again.
We can all climb down and play –
while the pirates sail away.

Yo, ho, ho! Hip, hip, hooray!
The pirates have all gone away.

ABOUT THE AUTHOR

John Barclay is a writer, entertainer and performance poet based in Dorset. A former company speechwriter, he retired early to Wareham, where for six years he contributed a monthly column to the Purbeck Gazette. He appeared regularly with the Rex Players (sometimes as MC) and wrote material for their shows.

He has developed 'Poetry a la Carte', in which he performs his own and other poems chosen by the audience from a menu. He has won local poetry slams and he became the Poole Word & Book Festival's Poet in Residence in 2004. In 2005, he brought out a book of poems 'The Blood of Others'. This is now out of print but a selection of pieces will be included in 'Poems for Adults', which will follow this publication. In 2012, he published a travel memoir *Surface Male - Round the World Without Flying.*

www.johnbarclayink.com